BEAUTIFUL
IRELAND

Published in Ireland by
Gill and Macmillan Ltd
Goldenbridge
Dublin 8
With associated companies in
Auckland, Dallas, Delhi, Hong Kong,
Johannesburg, Lagos, London, Manzini,
Melbourne, Nairobi, New York, Singapore,
Tokyo, Washington
© Photographs, 1990, Colour Library Books Ltd, Godalming, Surrey, England
© Text, 1990 Gill and Macmillan
Colour separation by Hong Kong Graphic Arts Ltd, Hong Kong
Printed and bound in Italy by New Interlitho
ISBN 0 7171 1772 3

BEAUTIFUL IRELAND

Gill and Macmillan

One of the most famous scenic roads in Ireland runs west from the small town of Dingle, Co Kerry, towards the promontory of Slea Head, the most westerly point in the country. It is a majestic coastal road cut into the side of the mountains, offering some of the most spectacular marine views anywhere in the world – below you the churning sea; in the middle distance the Blasket Islands; and beyond them nothing except the broad Atlantic Ocean to take you all the way to America.

But in addition to this famous coast road, there is another. It is an older road which runs up the side of the mountain rather than round its base. It is very narrow. Grass grows up the middle and there is barely enough room for the cars to pass. It travels uphill for about two kilometres, offering no views other than those of the mountains themselves. Then suddenly it turns left and falls away downhill towards Dunquin, the little village beside Slea Head. The view is a riot of sky, ocean, islands and headlands. It is as if all creation lay at your feet. The conventional views of Slea Head and the Blaskets – so beautiful in themselves – seem banal in contrast to this stunning panorama.

This is the secret of beautiful Ireland. Once you think you have exhausted all its possibilities, it throws up new and unexpected delights. From Killarney in the south to the Giant's Causeway in the north; from Galway Bay to Dublin city, there is a profusion of sights to see and historical places to visit. And it's not just the obvious places – the ones in all the guide books – that make Ireland a delight, but all the out-of-the-way places that you can discover for yourself, sometimes without even trying!

One of the reasons for this is that Ireland is a small country with a small population. And yet it has an astonishing variety of scenery and character. It isn't crowded, yet it has a good, modern transport infrastructure so that travel – whether by road, rail or even by air – is easy and trouble-free. The south-west is dominated by the majestic mountains of Kerry and Cork with Killarney the jewel at its centre. The west of Ireland encompasses Counties Clare, Galway and Mayo with fabled Connemara on the north shore of Galway Bay the centrepiece of this region. Donegal in the north-west is one of the lesser known but most beautiful corners of Ireland, with mountains, glens and some of the cleanest, most unspoilt beaches in Europe. And so on through the lush countryside of the north-east, the river valleys and uplands of the east and the rolling hills, rich farmland and sandy beaches of the sunny south-east.

And even with all that, the great heartland of Ireland away from the coast has yet to be explored. The Shannon – the longest river in Britain or Ireland – and the wonderful daisy-chain of lakes in the north-central part of the country form a network for fishing and boating unrivalled in Europe. Indeed, even in the south-east the beautiful river valleys of the Barrow, the Nore, the Slaney and the Suir are a particularly lovely part of that lesser known Ireland which is always just around the corner.

Much of the delight of Ireland comes from its antiquity. There are impressive survivals from the ancient world all over the country – notably the incredible passage grave, which is over 5,000 years old, at Newgrange in the Boyne Valley. In the last thirty years it has been brilliantly excavated and restored by archaeologists. Irish towns and cities, too, are as old as many on the continent of Europe. In 1988, Dublin celebrated its millennium while Berlin celebrated its 750th birthday. At Cashel, the ancient seat of the kings of Munster overlooks the lush plains of Tipperary. In the early Christian period it was turned into an ecclesiastical centre. It is now one of the most dramatic and historic places in Ireland. Everywhere in Ireland, the drama and beauty of the past is at your fingertips.

So welcome to *Beautiful Ireland,* the small country with the big smile. Once you've been here you'll want to return again and again.

above and below: The Giant's Causeway is the most spectacular evidence of volcanic activity in these islands. It lies along the Antrim coast, where the basalt plateau terminates in cliffs, producing a picturesque landscape.

overleaf: A cliff-top view above Great Stookan with the Mishowen Peninsula in the distance.

left: Carrick-a-rede is connected to the mainland by a famous rope footbridge, which is erected each summer by local fishermen. *above:* Situated high on a sea-tunnelled rock on the road to Portrush are the extensive remains of Dunluce Castle. *right:* Built alongside what was to become an important medieval fortress and sea port Carrickfergus Castle represents the defensive function of one of the oldest towns in Ulster. *overleaf:* Belfast City Hall by night.

left: The Mourne Mountains comprise a cluster of over a dozen peaks reaching their greatest height in Slieve Donard, which is the highest mountain in Northern Ireland.

top right: A view from Crocknafeoia Wood of the Mourne Mountains. *above:* The Mourne Mountains as seen from the Spelga Dam.

above: Gosford Castle, Co Armagh, was built in Norman style for Archibald Acheson, the second Earl of Gosford. Work was commenced in 1819. *right:* Drum Manor Forest Park, near Cookstown, Co Tyrone, was the demesne of the Earls of Castlestewart.

left: Inner Lake, in Dartry Forest, Co Monaghan, was once part of the Dartry Demesne. *above:* Lough Erne, Co Fermanagh, a tranquil stretch of water from Enniskillen to Belleek, is a haven for both the fisherman and antiquary. *right:* Lough Neagh, Co Armagh, is the largest lake in these islands, having an area of 153 square miles. It receives the waters of the Upper Bann and is drained by the Lower Bann.

*: A breathtaking view of Downhill *and. right:* Benevenagh, whose scenery ust have inspired the traditional Irish elody 'The Derry Air', said to have en composed by an itinerant Irish rpist. *below:* Castlerock, Co ndonderry

above: Bringing the hay home in the Gap of Mamore, Co Donegal. *below and right:* The Donegal coastline is full of deserted beaches and quiet bays which can be suddenly transformed if the weather turns. *right:* A quiet settlement nestles on the shores of Donegal Bay.

overleaf: A golden sunset on Trawbreaga Bay.

left: A spectacular aerial view of the beach at Moneygold, located north of Grange, Co Sligo. *above:* Benbulben dominates the geography of the region. An inspiration to W B Yeats, this splendid example of a table-top mountain is also of great interest to botanists for its rare alpine flora and to the historian as the site of the death of Diarmuid, hero of 'The Pursuit of Diarmuid and Grainne'.

below and lower right: Ashford Castle, on the banks of Lough Corrib, a mock castle built for Sir Arthur Edward Guinness, has become one of Ireland's most prestigious hotels. *right:* the most outstanding features that remain of Cong Abbey are the three exquisite doorways in Romanesque/Early Gothic style.

overleaf: The statue of Saint Patrick keeps a watchful eye over Clew Bay. Croagh Patrick is a pilgrim centre, now a location for gold prospectors.

above: Ashleagh Falls is located near Leenane, Co Galway, the location for the film 'The Field', based on the play by J B Keane. *left:* Clifden, 'capital of Connemara', is a small fishing port on Clifden Bay providing an ideal base for those interested in exploring some of the loveliest regions of the West. *right:* The ruins of St Patrick's Church, a holy well and stations can be found on Downpatrick Head, Co Mayo. Just off the head is spectacular Doontristy – an isolated cliff rock. *overleaf:* Making hay in Mayo

top left and above: The central features of Connemara are the peaks of the Twelve Bens. Visible throughout the region they have been a source of inspiration to generations of landscape painters. *right:* Kingstown Bay located west of Clifden. *overleaf:* An evening scene at Westport Bay near Murrisk, Co Mayo.

left: Resembling a fjord, Killary Harbour is the drowned river valley of the Erriff River. *above and below:* Fishing boats on the quay in Roundstone, Connemara.

overleaf: Traditional stone walls are a common sight around Cornamona and Lough Corrib, Co Galway.

above: Very much part of the attraction of Connemara is the thatched cottage, here nestling snugly in the peaceful environs of Leenane. *right:* The beauty of mountain and river is captured at Ballinahinch, Co Galway.
left: The meadowland looks out over Ballinakill Bay.
overleaf: The rapids on the Owenriff River, Co Galway.

left: Enjoying an afternoon's golfing in Monaghan. *below:* The sun glitters on Lough Ramar, Co Cavan. *right:* Castle Island, for centuries seat of MacDermot of Moylurg is one of the islands located on Lough Key, Forest Park, Co Roscommon, once part of the Rockingham estate.
overleaf: Gorse, or furze, is abundant on Cooley Peninsula, Co Louth.
following page: Once an important centre for Paganism, Tara, according to legend, is where St Patrick lit the first Paschal Fire.

ese pages: The river Liffey runs through
he heart of Dublin. *top left:* Queen Maeve
ridge, leads on to Arran Quay with the
our Courts in the background. *lower left:*
esigned by James Gandon, the Four
ourts was extensively destroyed by
xplosives in 1922. The exterior is
ominated by a copper-covered lantern
ome and statues of Moses, Justice and
Iercy, Wisdom and Authority. *right:*
'Connell Bridge, formerly known as
arlisle Bridge, was built in 1791. *above:*
he Halfpenny Bridge, properly known as
ne Metal Bridge, takes its name from the
oll that was once charged to cross it.
verleaf: An aerial view of Dublin's city
entre.

left: The Bank of Ireland was built as a House of Parliament between 1729 and 1739. The principal showpiece of the building today is 'Pearce's House of Lords' containing valuable tapestries and a priceless Dublin Glass chandelier. *top right:* The General Post Office, in O'Connell Street. It was from there the 1916 insurgents proclaimed the Irish Republic. *above:* Portobello House once served as a hotel for travellers on the Grand Canal.

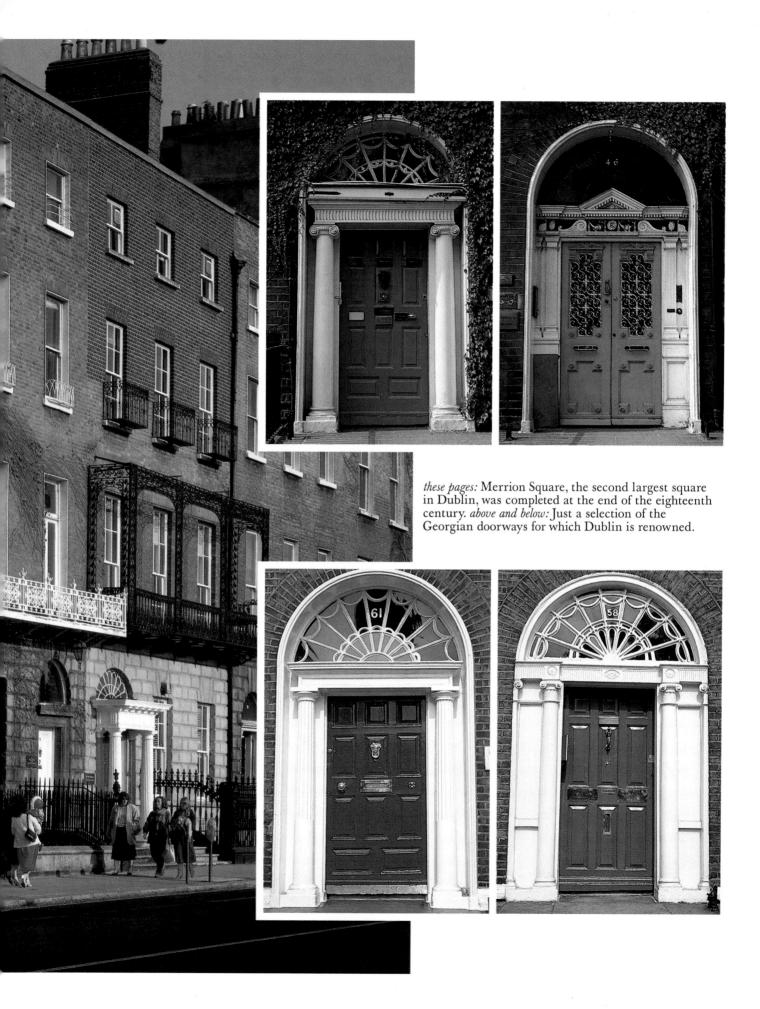

these pages: Merrion Square, the second largest square in Dublin, was completed at the end of the eighteenth century. *above and below:* Just a selection of the Georgian doorways for which Dublin is renowned.

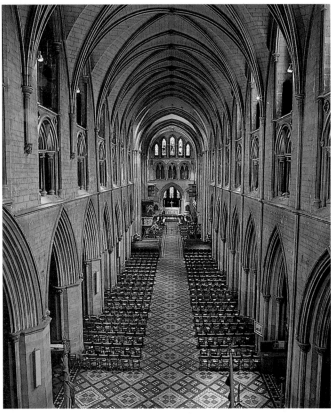

this page: Chiefly associated with Dean Jonathan Swift, St Patrick's Cathedral's three-hundred-foot-long interior makes it the longest church in Ireland.

left: The magnificent stairwell of Dublin's City Hall. *above:* the stairwell in the National Gallery of Ireland. The gallery was opened in 1864 and houses collections from European and Irish artists.

above: Trinity College's most photographed and familiar entrance. Founded in 1592 by Elizabeth I, the college remained essentially Protestant until the 1960s. Its most remarkable treasure is the Book of Kells. *left:* The Campanile in the Quadrangle of Trinity College. *right:* The library in the Long Room, Trinity College, Dublin.

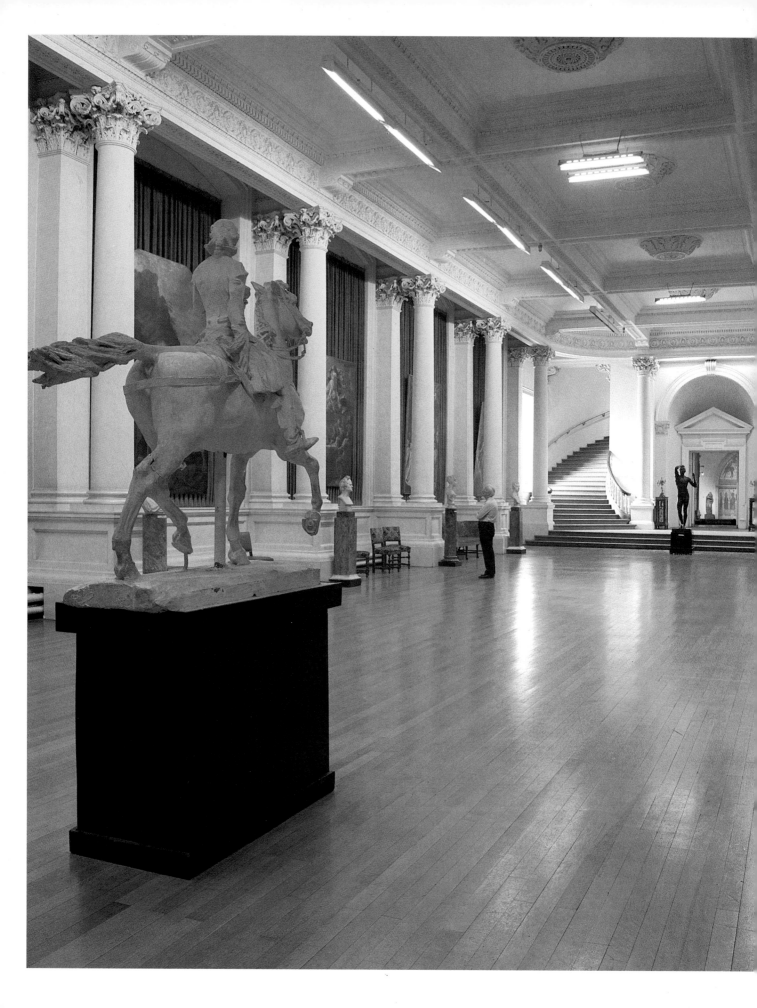

left and above: The National Gallery of Ireland contains over six thousand paintings – however, only a selection are on view. *top right:* Visitors are welcome to view the magnificent State Apartments in Dublin Castle. Little remains of the Castle's medieval origins and its present condition is due to extensive restoration work.

top left: Marsh's Library, built in 1707 is the oldest public library in Ireland. *above:* The National Library has important collections of books, manuscripts, drawings, prints and historical archives. *right:* The National Museum houses an impressive array of Irish antiquities.

left: Bruxelles pub, Harry Street, Dublin. *above and below:* The Long Hall, Georges Street, is an old Dublin pub complete with 'snug'. After a hard day working or sightseeing there is nothing nicer than to relax with a pint of Guinness or perhaps some of Ireland's famous whiskey.

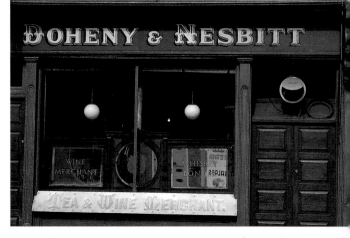

this page: Eighteenth-century Dublin is reflected in the capital's traditional shop fronts and public houses.

left: The Phoenix Park on Dublin's Northside is one of the largest and most magnificent city parks in Europe. Covering 1,752 acres, it has remained the habitat for deer. Within its boundaries is Áras an Uachtaráin, the residence of the President of the Republic of Ireland. *above:* Visitors to Dublin can enjoy a leisurely stroll along the banks of the Royal Canal.

top left: An aerial view of Glendalough, Co Wicklow and *above:* Its famous
Round Tower.
overleaf: Falls on the Glenmacnass River near Laragh, Co Wicklow.

left: Hook Head is a long narrow peninsula known for its beautiful corals. *above* Kilmore Quay is thirteen miles from Rosslare. It is a well-known deep-sea angling centre.

overleaf: A view from the Rock of Danamase, near Portlaois, Co Laois.

top left: A tranquil scene on the River Blackwater, Co Meath. *above:* Birr Castle still remains the seat of the Parsons family, whose present head represents the fourteenth generation to live there.
right: The castle of the Butlers, Cahir, Co Tipperary, was erected in 1142, taken by Elizabeth I's Earl of Sussex and surrendered to Cromwell in 1650.
overleaf: The Monastery of Clonmacnoise, Co Offaly.

left: The Round Tower on the Bay of Ardmore dates from the 9th century, perhaps one of the earliest in Ireland. *top right:* The gentle slopes of Slieve Kilmalta rise to nearly 2,300 feet near Knockfune. *above:* The Rock of Cashel stands majestically on a limestone outcrop, overlooking the plains of Tipperary.

this page: A highly skilled workforce produces the famous Waterford lead crystal for export all over the world.

overleaf: The gently undulating landscape around Knocknanash, Co Waterford.

left: Rising seven hundred feet above the Atlantic Ocean, the Cliffs of Moher extend for five miles along the county Clare coast. *above:* The Ennistymon river, Cullenagh. *below:* A cove near Tramore, Co Waterford.

this page: Kinsale, Co Cork, is perhaps the most charming harbour town in the country. Situated on the Bandon Estuary it is of interest to the historian as the site of the Battle of Kinsale in 1601 when the plans for attack were intercepted and the combined forces of the Spanish and Irish fell into disarray and were forced to retreat. Kinsale once more fell into English hands.
overleaf: On the shores of Adrigole Bay

this page: Blarney Castle and the Blarney Stone. Blarney Castle was built in 1446 by Cormac Laidir MacCarthy. Below the battlements is the famous Blarney Stone, the kissing of which allegedly grants the gift of eloquence.
overleaf: The fertile plains of Co Cork.

top left and left: Cork city, the third largest city in Ireland, is beautifully situated on the River Lee. Cork's medieval origins may be attributed to a monastery built by St Finbarr. Later on, like many other Irish monasteries it was subjected to attack by the Vikings. King Dermot MacCarthy surrendered to the Anglo-Normans but it was not enough and the town was declared a dependency of the English Crown in 1185. *above:* Father Matthew Memorial Church and Parliament Bridge.

overleaf: St Colman's Cathedral dominates the harbour of Cobh, formerly known as Queenstown, not far from Cork city.

left and overleaf: Among the numerous beauty spots of County Kerry are the Lakes of Killarney. *above:* A waterfall on the Owenreagh River.
overleaf: A resting spot on the shores of one of the Lakes of Killarney.

left: Dingle, is a charming market town and fishing port on the southside of the Corca Dhuibhne Peninsula. *below:* Castle Street, the busy thoroughfare of the county's capital. *right:* Perhaps the most striking feature of Killarney is St Mary's Cathedral.

this page: Muckross House was built in 1843 and houses a folk museum, where the skills of traditional weaving may still be seen.
overleaf: Muckross Abbey, one of Ireland's finest Gothic abbeys, was founded in the 1440s for the Franciscan order.

ft: Sheep grazing on the hilly farmland around the village of nascaul, Co Kerry.

above: Clouds obscure the view of the peaks of Caherconree Mountain, in the Slieve Mish range, Co Kerry.

left: A view across the beautiful strand of Smerwick Harbour looking towards Kilmalkedar with the Three Sisters in the background. *right:* Dingle Peninsula. The rugged beauty of the Corca Dhuibhne Peninsula conceals a wealth of prehistoric and early historic remains.

top left and above: Just a selection of the scenery that Dingle has to offer. *right:* Coumeenoole Strand.

overleaf: Doon Point, located near the mouth of the River Shannon.